ATTACK

AND

COUNTERATTACK

Who doesn´t know this: Is Lost

Luis E. Martinez

First published 2011

To my children: Roxiré and Aldo

CONTENTS

ESTABLISHED ORDER

An attack can originate from almost any motivation and in pursuit of almost any target, giving the case that these generally are preceded by what is considered a sufficient reason to warrant such action. In most cases, such attacks are offensive, but can also be defensive, and this is mainly generated in response to a previous attack and therefore more applicable to the context of counter-attack, as there may be an initial attack with defensive criterion, which often are of a preventive attack, and are generated when an enemy or ally counterparts, there are situations that would warrant a correction or neutralization, in an attempt to avoid greater evils or reckoning.

The reasons that could justify an attack or counterattack, sometimes can be very confusing, and a lot of disordered factors take advantage of this to ensure unscrupulously exploit, which is equivalent to that of "fish in troubled waters", and obviously the goal of factors of order would consist in setting the base clearly the true causes of the situations of which usually take advantage the disordered ones to try to justify what would be an attack or counterattack against the established order or seeks to impose.

The attack methods and factors are not really many: among them we could mention the conventional war, guerrilla war, coup, popular elections, civil war, acts of terrorism, cyber attacks, subliminal attack, etc. To these you could add The so called revolutions, but reality these are inherent to the methods or factors discussed above, for it would also be called a revolution to either one of them, even the circumstances created by a popular election, to which they will call peaceful and democratic revolution, but even still: they

4

don't stop being equal to or worse than the factors which involved violence or fighting force, more by the consequences than the causes, as in conventional warfare or guerrilla warfare for example it practically is left open the possibility to retaliate with force methods, with no greater motivation than just having used them in such circumstances to gain power, or pretend to.

But in the case of so-called peaceful and democratic revolution, there are major flaws in the system, interpretation of legality, legitimacy and validity, making it wrongly, the disordered ones are covered by what apparently is the established order and accepted by all, mainly by factors of order, this gives rise to for example, if an extreme factor access to power through popular election, can later perform all types of abuses against the factors of order and even disordered factors and could not be neutralized in such purpose, because according to existing legal aberrations, to the disordered ones in power are protected by the facto of having obtained the greatest number of votes than any other factor.

Even so, the disordered ones prefer to change the rules because actually being people of order is not their condition, and in any case, they are severely disadvantaged compared to factors of order, also to be such, especially since sooner or later it could leave in legal disadvantage, the fact of losing electoral majority or other factors, they do that if for example they access to the legislature by a majority vote proportion of the population, then this rule may be changed and impose a new rule, where power not necesarely being decided by proportional voting majority of the population, but by the vote share of only a few sectors, while ensuring that these are where they have preserved the greatest number of followers, sometimes making the vote only of a few voters, get a parliamentary majority over other factors with the highest number of votes and therefore more popular support.

Apart from this change of rules, they use many other methods of attack and neutralization against order factors such as the kidnapping of all public authorities, including the most neuralgic, such as the judiciary, where they get their fix for all judicial decisions, namely the prosecutorial and judicial court, these reinforce them with mastery of the comptroller and public advocacy. To round off the internal domain, they use violent groups that violate the factors and intimidate opponents, including dissidents who are removed from their causes, fraudulent electoral mechanisms in which the opponents have no more say, "black list" of opponents to their causes with the intent to exercise extortion and blackmail depriving them job opportunities and investment, etc.

As if this were not enough, they try to become a significant international lobby, consisting of nations with regimes of the same link, which provide mutual support in defense of any sanctions admissions arrangements and agencies that ensure a better international order or at least it appear to be so , which makes the existentialism of the citizens of the countries where the disordered get to exercise dominium, be very traumatic, even for the vast majority of supporters of these regimes, for the support shown almost always is a product of manipulation , extortion and blackmail, and also because most of these followers, is represented by the citizens of greater intellectual and socio-economic insecurity.

The guard does not always originate in the related international lobby, but also of great ideological opponents of the disordered ones, because there are serious limitations to sovereignty and self determination of peoples, and legal basis for access to power, becoming at times all international lobby, in one of the biggest obstacles that prevent citizens of order, to get rid of extremists, so in case of seeking a peaceful vote, it is impossible for the threats, government manipulation, blatant use of resources of state under unfavorable electoral rules and exclusive control of these ones and if you try the way of force, then it would act the international mechanisms, especially the sub-regional with measures of exclusion and international isolation.

This attitude makes international factors, the accomplices of the tyrannical regimes whose only credential of legitimacy, is represented by the coming to power through an electoral majority, almost completely ignoring the aberrations committed by these regimes, as it would always have the mitigating of this electoral majority as sufficient reason not to act against them, even so: if any steps against these ones the extremists would appeal to the factor of national sovereignty, and this also represents an almost impossible to beat barrier to most cases, or perhaps it is effective, it would be after the extremists had devastated the country where they performed with the sequel of human and structural calamities that they had left.

To continue this type of situation it would be necessary to warn very severely to international accomplices factors of disordered systems, on the traumatic situations they are exposed to, if they do not desist from providing unconditional support to any regime, although it would be occupied by factors that achieved an electoral majority, the development of these apply more as a tyranny than a regime of order.

Among the most serious consequences that would bring the aberrations committed by both the tyrannical regime and its accomplices, would be the fact that it would be given legitimacy to a very radical defense factors, as no other way would be left out but these, and in macro terms, they would not be the ideal ones at   first-hand, but if they are, as the peaceful ways are collapsed, as the fact where all internal decisive powers are handled at will of the disordered ones, at par with international factors of weight, would be in complicity with them.

Obviously the disordered factors act at will, if on them there is a higher power that will make them desist from their purpose, even a relatively minor force weight but very forcefully, as in the case of suicide bombers and even is a method widely used by extremists to achieve their aims, but obviously the factors of order one would use these only in extreme situations and against different targets, mainly only of material type, trying to avoid human losses, especially the innocent type, also trying to prevent suicide factor as such, and in the best of cases take advantage of the context of high risk attacker, but not necessarily suicidal, and this does not differ largely from the conventional soldier, because when they are involved in combat there is a high risk of being discharged, but they are not necessarily suicidal.

Apart from using the term high risk attacker by the order, we will better use the term kamikaze, because in essence these attackers were of high risk, but not necessarily suicidal, and inclusive they are very few testimonies where they would have acted as suicides, but would be more for personal reasons and without the consent of their superiors. The kamikazes of the order would have as priorities, the power outage and if this does not create a withdraw of purpose in the extremist sector, then it will be proceeded against the leadership of these ones, and for all purposes: it would act under the premise of absolute principle of self-defense.

One of the strategic advantages held by disordered ones about the order, is represented by the fact that they take advantage of two factors of attack are, one peaceful: which is represented by the electoral factor, and another of force, which is represented by violent factors of almost any kind, in contrast, the factors of order practice almost exclusively the electoral votes factor, this means that if the onset of force by the disordered ones is very strong, the sum of attack factors ends deciding in favor of them, and like that it would continue almost indefinitely, until by errors of the same disordered ones, they end up collapsing, or until the same factors of order decide also to appeal to force factors, as a strategic factor in seeking to impose over the disordered ones.

It does not result easy to factors of order, to function in the use of force factors, as since in itself: this one is surrounded by a stigma of rejection by the majority of the population, almost with no other motivation than the consequences it generates, what makes it preferable to non-violent or peaceful factors, apart from this, disordered factors seek to deepen the rejection against the factors of order, using precisely the concepts that are related to them, but they are cleverly saddled with the ones of the order, which is a typical condition of so-called fascism, but broadly applied as the intelligentsia of the defeat, that is: to use in their own favor and against the order factors, those factors where the disorder results defeated by the order.

It is inconvenient to take as reference of government, almost only and exclusively, at least substantially to the lagging sectors of the population, so, they are very unpredictable and unstable, and also that by nature they have a great tendency to prefer a disordered leadership and particularly as it dismissed or relegated to a second level, the factors that really should exercise the major governmental reference, which is represented by the factors of greatest intellectual capacity and socio-economic, but so, all these circumstances represent some of the reasons that the disordered ones get to misrepresent that get messy, and generate the force that somehow or other they keep, and would continue keeping until precisely, are the citizens of greater intellectual capacity, who direct the destiny of each country and therefore the whole system.

The fight against disorderly factors should not happen only when they get to exercise government control, but it is necessary to combat them by any means, and in any event, as the damage they generate is usually devastating, and obviously preventing against them avoid these ills, but while there is an established order where in some way or another it gives them a place of management, either by access to power through electoral vote or by factors of force, inevitably they were seeking to take advantage of this circumstance to achieve its objectives, what makes partially that the blame for the existence of the disordered ones, fall upon the same factors of order, but not because it is the intention of these, but by the ignorance of many adverse parameters that exist in the established order, but given the wrong effect, being perhaps the most significant one, the fact of allowing that any individual with no more credentials than gathering an electoral majority, can exercise the governmental regency, especially the main ones.

Another one of the parameter that are very adverse, is represented by the failure to possess a status or only contexts on the real concepts or ideal context, of some indicators of geopolitical order, as sometimes for example, they speak about seeking the major prosperity and wealth for the citizens, but other times it is said that to be wealthy is a something bad, just as we have established as measures of good government management, maintaining a positive rate of economic growth or low index of inflation, but the disordered ones fake to their pleasure the figures for these indicators, with no further possibility of doing an audit where we could demonstrate the falsity of them, or where they speak of a high popularity of some leader or as a universal synonym of acceptance, but they do not take into account the precarious condition of popularity of the citizens, where sometimes there even occurs an inverse proportionality where "at a greater popularity of the regime and its leaders, less popularity of citizens."

It also plays a fundamental role, the no existence of an only context of democracy, and this is so pathetic that sometimes some of the contexts of these are completely opposite and contradictory, but equally everyone is accepted as a context of democracy, and it's here: exactly where they should begin efforts to reorganizing the system, that is the establishment of a unique context of the ideal regime, simultaneous to this it must be superseded any other kind of ideology, but accepting the freedom of dissident thought, taking into consideration that they must be negated technical and irrefutably by the principles established by the order, which gives greater strength to these ones, many proponents of the democratic ideal, best applied to followers of the center ideal, and this if it has more uniform context.

Lots of people play in maintaining the validity of his " way of thinking" or "particular philosophy," and this would not be mostly problematic, if said ideas were in synchronized with the thinking of existing logic maximum or an improvement of these, and indeed there are parameters that require the force of an only order in the system, and these were derived from the rigorous legal system, which is common to all sectors and factors, since the natural laws act identically and only in any latitude, and likewise, are impossible to dodge, as it has implicit even the capital penalty in case of not being managed according to the parameters set by them.

This requires a distinction between the political and religious elements as factors of governance, as there are precepts of a religious nature colliding with natural laws, which represent a kind of homicide by those who promote them and force its execution, and kind a of suicide by those who are governed by them, yet, in the case where religious precepts are synchronized in harmony with the political element it is allowed the relative management on separate of both elements at least that is the case in the Christian religion.

Some religions have established, not only to ignore some parameters of natural laws, but also have even established to attack other religions under the simple reasons of supremacy, forcing any other religion to be kept in a status of counterattack regarding the first one, so that the attack for simple supremacy does nothing but represent a cannibalistic attitude, as for the simple criterion of supremacy is not an absolute principle of operation. Given this, one can say that sooner or later it will disappear the religions that has established to attack the others by the simple criterion of supremacy, and that will happens from the moment that the followers of these religions, understand the inconvenient of continue and expose to counter-attacking of the non attacking religions, as they would be defending a totally illogical principal, that is: merely cannibal, as it is no permitted to deliberate reasons beyond his own.

The eradication of the attacking religions would be even more accelerated: if they also include within their precepts, an operation contrary to natural laws, then not only would they be exposed to counter-attack by non attacking religions, but also to suicide which represents not sticking strictly to the natural laws, or attempt of murder when the religious precepts and even political pretend to impose themselves through forced way. All this allows to establish that the Christian religion will be the only ones that finally exist as for the non attacking religions, is the only one whose political element is strictly adhered to the rigorous legal system, this allows also to establish: that the Christian religion is the only true one and others result to be false religions

Since there is the intelligentsia of the defeat, the factors to fight back would not only be those who openly declare themselves as non-Christians, but also those which infiltrate or make think as Christians or factors of order, but despite the furtive circumstance, they are very abundant the parameters by which they can be detect, being the most predominant, when they attack the traditional factors of order and because they show an operation based on the parameter of only fighting evil, ignoring or neglecting to a second place, the parameters of practicing only what is good, and not to practice what is evil, being these last two ones together with the parameter of practicing what is essentially good which makes up the principle of absolute order, or absolute context of good.

Obviously the operation to develop would not only be that of exclusively counter attack to the factors of disorder, but instead would be seeking to withdraw purposes by the disordered ones, and better yet, to procure a conversion to factors of order, this operation will be regulated by the initiatives of attack of the factors of disorder and those of counterattack from the order factors, bearing in mind that global leadership, must be represented by the citizens of major intelligentsia.

Summarizing the above: it makes clear the possibility of an environment or system where they would be doing things the best way possible, because the whole operation would be based on legal rigor of the system, which would leave out of place the cumbersome that it sometimes results to deliberate or be guided by the uncertainty of any ideas, that although in occasions that are very well thought out, it would not be the same as when you have a solid matrix, such as to be guided by strict laws that provide nature, also by the absolute supremacy that intelligence posses over any other factor, which allows to separate significantly the flood of ideas of almost all type, that are commonly exposed by the factors intellectual intermediate and larger, covered by the allowed free will , and it is not that they will disappear, but it is necessary to debug previously both qualitative and quantitative, and choose which would be the best of them.

In the environment of ideas and reasons that have allowed the force of factors frankly disturbing, these will begin to disappear by the simple fact that different sectors, including virtually the entire system will set the inconvenience and rejection of such factors of disturbance as only it will be permitted a single regent factor, which is represented by intelligence, in this way there will be no place for promotion with government criteria, of factors such as force and simple electoral majority, and within these, the operational factors such as the simple revenge, patriotism, honesty, charisma, popularity, etc.., or because the promoters would not apply as intellectual factors of a top-level or because the reasons do not apply or have lost force.

MONOPOLY OF FORCE OR VIOLENCE.

When speaking about monopoly of force, also you almost speaks monopoly of violence, but because the context of violence is somewhat ambiguous, it is good to establish differences: from this we get that the term violence may represent:

A- The simple use of force against any foreign or own objective, and even against oneself.

B- on-limited use of force in cases where this is exercised with the greatest extent than that agreed, or in appearance, whether it did not warrant to be of greater magnitude, or that the magnitude was necessary, since the goal did warrant it, this implies that the use of force relatively with no greater weight, would not apply as violence.

C- When a dominant force is exercised on some target without the consent of this one or the established order, some cases of consented force as in masochism, the same it is just applied as violence.

D- The most dissimilar cases of legal type where there are parameters of use of force, but the limitations are set at the discretion of legislators or presidents of different legislative bodies, or taking into account the existential factor or in the same way completely ignoring this, this means that sometimes the context of violence depends only on those who also possess the monopoly context of a country, a governing body or related to the etymology, or the whim of any group or individual, and obviously the lack of rigidity in what would be a single order agreed in the context of violence, it represents one of the factors that makes violence or what is supposed to be violence, have much effect, as almost any one reserves the right exclusive or rhetorical , to consider what is or is not violence.

Having all this: we can say that violence represents both a factor of peace and order or also of disorder, and the existence of contradictions or inaccuracies in this context, implies severe trauma to the citizens, that precisely could be avoided, if we manage to establish an irrefutable criterion of what would or not be violence, and indeed there is already a unique and compelling approach that allows to establish not necessarily the context of violence as such, but indeed one of its antonyms, which is represented by the context of freedom and From this one, it is automatically defined the violence, for what goes against freedom, becomes part of the context of violence, not only in regards to the context of violence as such but also as actually being violence , seeks to impose itself as possible.

16

This would eliminated the monopoly of violence and any permissive general or sectorial form to exercise it, since all that threatens against freedom is something to be condemned, which would reduce the practice of violence only to common criminals, almost regardless of the type of legislation and how severe they may be, you always find those who will risk themselves to practice it, and as per high-level offenders, especially those that abound in the geopolitical environment, will have virtually shut down all operational possibilities, because the factors they use to do this, have practically become obsolete.

The unique and compelling context of freedom is defined as "the ability to operate discreetly within the range of life" this way: taking all vital parameters of the individual, both organic as outsiders to the same factors that are essential for their existentiality, would represent the main controlling factor, which permits to establish the different discretion or indiscretion that are operating according to the largest possible force of vital factor or affecting this one.

Within the parameters of the individual organic life, are the sensitivity of the senses and that one regulated by the nerve system, where an alteration in the visual or auditory sensitivity, for example, or that affects the nervous system, already represents a violent attack to the vital factor , the same occurs when they are attacked some parameters that are not firmly established the mechanisms that regulate them or from where they come, like love, ego, anger, pride, vanity, some parameters of sexual desire, the desire of addiction, etc., the functioning of vital organs, and the factors that are necessary to sustain them, etc., and any other vital factor, having the

17

particularity all of them to remain in effect or operation, provided that they remain within minimum and maximum supply, complacency or exposure, taking into consideration that many of them are cyclical and of almost immediate attention.

COMMON FACTOR

The need, desire or convenience of a counterattack is a common factor to all sectors, that is: they all struggle to survive, but not all counterattack is feasible, as it depends on the factors involved such an initiative, especially the power of the operators and objectives that they would get or lose, this fact becomes very traumatic when their own vital factors were found on high risk, then it would be appropriate to defer a possible counterattack, seeking a more suitable environment for this, which may contain a greater offensive or defensive capacity, and or a decrease in these same factors in the opposing attacker, it would also be at stake eventual successful negotiation to the parties who avoid what would be the unpredictable consequences of a confrontation. When negotiating possibilities do not exist or they exist but would be unconvincing, and along with this increases the existential danger itself, it generate situations of forced digitizing, which represents a factor that forces an imminent taking of decisions of the yes or not type motivated to that the adversity leaves no alternative.

Some factors of attack that gained great importance in the past have almost completely outdated, as the desire of conquest, in these cases, the established order allowed that circumstance, but then the established order itself, was paving the way, until finally the established order is totally opposed to the old practice, but did not disappear completely the desire of conquest, at least open and consented as in the past, although in a very small scale, there are factors that seek allegations, which allow what would be fully justified counterattack with the purposes of territorial annexation, conquest of this separatist approach, which in one way or another have led to recent changes in the world map.

The fact that only citizens of greater intellectual capacity, are called to exercise governmental supremacy implies that a large sector of those who believed themselves with the right to exercise governmental positions: will disappear, as they do not qualify for them and nothing would help them to compel effort in it, as these would be legitimate targets of counter attack by any factor that prefers the major order, and as per the intellectual factors, there would not be major problem, as for the context of intelligence itself, they are the best trained to avoid them, along that they are not very abundant in these intellectual elites and in change: Generally, indeed they abound middle and lower government positions, but the choosing of these minor positions would not represent either something traumatic, as they would be under the regency of intellectual leaders, and not of any universe and disordered as up to now.

This system would be very similar to the polling stations that exist today, only that the heads of these schools or governing body of the new order would be made only by intellectual elites, in this way, the internal rivalry in an attempt to seize power, would reach limits very peaceful, because they would not take place the violent ones, what might be called the internal struggle for power, would be relegated to the desire of the elite intellectual factors in achieving the best credentials for operational soundness in favor of the population, and not the art of going around collecting votes or electoral support as far and widely, is this operation, and less more, to situations of violent attacks of all kinds, including coup d'etat, guerrilla warfare, revolutions or collateral of these known as terrorism.

In the political atmosphere there are several contexts of revolution, among these the one that represents a mere figure of combat, establishing a break against a regime or order, and the one that represents a form of government or established order, this being very typical on the left, and within its main features is the fact of becoming surrounded by a kind of "holy halo" and immaculate, where everything that is opposed to the revolution would represent a terrible blasphemy worthy of severe punishment against those who do oppose, allowing the leadership of them: all kinds of abuses in the name of the supposedly sacred revolution and almost unqualified acceptance of this fact, it represents one of the most severe operational failures of human beings, while it can be said that it has represented one of the most effective strategies of left extremism, to carry out their evil purposes.

Apart from the "holy halo" upon the revolution, they also do surround with it these leaders and their followers, commonly represented by intellectual and socio-economically disadvantaged sectors, forming a trio of atrocity and impunity that most of the time just disappear or become outdated by depletion of themselves, but rarely by effective counter-attacks of the order factors, although the factor of disorder represented by the right-wing ideology, it was more effective than the center in this area, especially as they use factors of force to neutralize them, but even so: the right side is another factor where freedom is strongly suppressed, and the mere use of force without a valid reason for maximum logic, may simply represent parameters of cannibalism, and it is precisely a part of what is pretended to avoid, so it is only left to counterattack the irregular ones, precisely to procure maximum logic factors: whether they are peaceful or of force.

The need for survival is a common factor to all individuals, and equally it is common the requirement to eat almost every day to satisfy that purpose, but not always readily available dietary factors, as sometimes it is even very traumatic to get them as similarly there are parasite factors, seeking food theft as such, or to get sheltering factors such as money, such theft is not always the classical and pursued figure of robbery, as such, but disorder factors make use of legal mechanisms as the method of expropriations to steal the means of production of factors of order or disorder itself, which increases existential cannibalism factors in the system.

The reasons the disordered ones argue to try to justify an attack of such expropriation, are usually the type of revenge, so that these attacks are actually raised as a counter attack, and they avail themselves by manipulation or ignoring the different orders established through history, and the force that they would even have or that would have lost, in this way: If some of them have been eradicated, cleverly they try to expose them as still in force, or as effectively eradicated but subject to retaliation, vindication and reckoning by factors that took the worst part, while they had or are still valid, this means that for them it has been useless, peace treaties, recognition of independence and sovereignty, armistice, inter acculturation, reconciliation, forgiveness, approaches, integration, efficiency of some individuals and ineptitude of others and so on.

Finally, in some way or another they seek to republish stories already expired, with the intention of slipping in as successors or heirs of old deeds and glory, and thus play a role of protagonic leader that makes them digestible to the population, as figures of supreme importance that deserved all the respect and obedience, and that to hinder them in their vindicating purposes would be a vile action, worthy of utter contempt, for allegedly the nation where operating need be taken to the place of honor deserved, and above all, because presumably the time would have already come to make justice in favor of the lingered citizens, victims of abuses committed by the Regents of the established orders that outraged them, and also bring exemplar punishment to the heirs or even representatives of these regimes of the past.

GROUNDS AND MEANS

You can say that one of the largest differences between common criminals and geopolitical offenders: it is the fact that except in cases where some of the first dedicate to the practice of fraud and theft, the rest of them practice their misdeeds exposing themselves openly as such, trying to make clear to their victims, what they actually are, and generally also, the violent and despicable that can be attack by them, in change geopolitical offenders: prefer to make use of the stealth factor that also posses the Common criminals that practice fraud, for presenting themselves publicly as the criminal they actually are, exposes them to face factors of justice very powerful in quantity and quality at local and global level, but even so, while they can be promoted publicly as perverse, As well they do, because it gives them a certain status of arbitrariness, impunity and supremacy between the evil ones, and they use it to show in some way or another their true condition.

You can say that everyone acts guided by some motive that justifies their behavior, and even in some cases of oppression or threat, where the individual may be forced to act against their will: this one seeks to justify his behavior, ranking his priority of survival or guarding of any other factor, for all this to happen, it is necessary a justification scheme, on both parties the attackers and the attacked, and not always the attackers achieve their goals, but sometimes they are obliged to desist from these, or are neutralized or eliminated during the rigors of the attack or a later counterattack from the attacked ones and/or their allies.

Patterns of attack and counterattack, are digital type as to the results that they can yield these two digital parameters could be summarized into one that represent winning and another that represents losing, and from there, the different synonyms and antonyms of these ones, which in turn has implied a criterion of supremacy for the dominant factor and ignominy for the loser or defeated. The factors arising from this can get to have connotations of great significance, where the winners would be worthy of great respect and consideration, at the same time it would make them worthy of the control of established order or sectorial in change the defeated factors, are sheltered circumstances of hardship, sometimes immersed in parameters of exclusion and despise, being exposed in some cases to executions, confinement, banishment, slavery, or simply trying to survive under the parameters of freedom, trying to earn a living in precarious circumstances.

This, it is not necessary to happen in combat or simple competition, but even, for example, by simply being born under certain parameters, life can be exquisite or disastrous, depending among other factors: on the type of race socioeconomic condition, physical appearance, among others, even dough, this kind of circumstance is generator after parameters of revenge, vindication, solidarity, resentments, etc. That changes a natural circumstance simple fact of being born, in conflict situations, premeditated aggravated and continued, that fortunately end up losing force or much of this, when some dominant factors begin to see the logic and illogic of the circumstances that are happening, and choose to desist from attacking and counter-attacking purposes.

In this way the reasons wielded with intent to maintain a dominant status, generally disappear, for reasons of maximum logic, including cases where, for example, some factors traditionally dominated, get important defeats over the dominant ones by force factors , and more than for these reasons of force, the circumstances are defined as it would be illogical to attack a factor that can offer a very forceful response, with an even greater magnitude as that of the attacking factor what makes that, apparently it would end up be imposing a harmonic correlation status or peaceful coexistence.

And they say, apparently because, although the order represents an absolute factor, it is also true that evil is a constant factor, and while the factors of order will not seek to cling to the status of all the order factor, which involves reducing evil to a minimum, there are always circumstances of disturbance in the system, remembering that the order whether, consists of three basic parameters, the first being: do what is essentially good, the second, do not do evil, and the third, fighting the evil, if not met these three parameters to its fullest, then it is not good enough, since the correlation between good and evil act inversely in proportion, that is: to greater goodness: less evilness, and to greater evilness: less goodness, only that the operating power of evil, is subject to the absolute context of goodness, and you can only achieve absolute power rate by a close correlation with God, for He is the only absolute factor in essence.

Seeking an established order without trauma, represents the desire of the factors of order, and even of the messy   type, only that these ones seek such an order using unscrupulous means, which is a paradox in the pursuit of perfect order, but until they are sufficiently decoded parameters that establish what would be the real coordinates of the ideal order, like it or not: there will always be trauma, as it remains open the possibility that where we want to do things the best you can, there would rise perturbing factors that will give effect to the occurrence of traumas, there are also factors essentially evil, whose status is to do evil, with no greater motivation than this attitude is a peculiar condition in them, and in this it is common the intervention of evil spiritual creatures.

No matter how perverse a human being is, they apparently do not have the capacity to develop parameters of evilness as deeply produced, as those observed in the most dissimilar situations where sometimes they do occur, and it is not that there isn't human beings evil enough , but in occasions' they seem to operate under the guidelines of evil spiritual leadership, since most of the evil attack is oriented to oppose the guidelines of the one true and only God to men, represented by apart from the perverse ones, by those what we might call : the spirit of antichrist, even for many high connoisseurs of Christian doctrine, they find it extremely difficult to decode some parameters where it will be generating disputes or attacks against it, which makes that much of the fight against evil, have to be taken from true knowledge about the Christian doctrine.

Using false vindication schemes falsely vindictive that occur in the political element, political leaders and ordinary citizens seeking to engage their supporters and eventual followers, in messy situations that are contrary to the guidelines of the Christian doctrine, sometimes taking advantage of the promotion of the Christian principle themselves, but this is done from the perspective of intellectuality of defeat posing as authentic Christians, then by disorderly practices, they try to identify more themselves more with the evil that the Christian ideal that they have been promoting or practicing. It is also true that when the environment allows them, the disordered ones make a frontal attack on religion, preferring not to share hegemony with the religious leadership, trying to eradicate the religious element itself if applicable.

In contrast, when the attacks are mainly from the religious element, there is no effort to eradicate political element, particularly because you do not need more evidence to prove the existence of this one, while the religious element requires parameters of furtive or discrete demonstration that oblige to believe in the existence of God without having more evidence, but it is indeed typical that they try to hijack a political element from the religious element, which is extremely traumatic, both in cases where doctrinal precepts of a religion are not in harmonic synchrony with the legal rigor of the system, or when they really are, but precisely by being contradictory political management from the religious element when there is no conviction of faith in all factors, then the same it is generated considerable trauma, this happens only with factors of Christian doctrine as the only legal rigor attached to the system.

The magnitude and the ideology entanglement in the political is such that it even has many political ideals that are still valid, some in direct conflict with other, as happens in the religious element, where dozens of religions attend of every kind and creed, only that in the case of the religious element, apart from the context of ideology as such, it is also necessary and sometimes of greater weight the existence of the principle of faith. Many geopolitical factors are determined to maintain the validity of the professed ideal, mostly by taking advantage of the accumulated wealth that they have certain political and religious tendency, which the perfect or most logical reason that can represent these trends, some even play in diametrically opposed scenarios, such as the cases of some leftist leaders on the one hand preach the convenience of a life of austerity, but on the other hand, are immersed in the virtues of capitalism and luxurious lives.

But what really gives more validity to the factors of order, is represented by the fact that the factors of order have not been very effective in debugging in the strongest possible way the existing ideological mess, in other words, until now the factors of order have not been sufficiently effective in developing or promoting the criteria of maximum logic, which simultaneously provide greater solidity to the top of the order, and set aside completely or almost completely the criteria for the disorder that uses both its own , as derived from the intelligentsia of defeat. Reasoned that the true context of politic or political element is defined as the complement of the religious element, it is necessary to achieve the ideal order, to establish guidelines of the rearranged system, through a close correlation between the doctrinal principles of the religious element and the political.

In the political environment it would be necessary to consider some modifications of existing paradigms, such as freedom of thought, as this represents the starting point for the elaboration and promotion of ideas, and it is not that you have to eradicate and less still disrespecting the freedom of thought, but this should be framed within both qualitative and quantitative parameters according to the ideals set forth, either existing or new.

In this respect, it must be taken care to place the ideas of maximum logic as a ruler factor, in the second place the ideas that offer lot of content on maximum logic but not in sufficiently or at least it would require further discussion to establish definitive criteria for this, so that they can be fully operational in the third place, ideas that if they would not be of the maximum logic, at least they provide satisfactory operational capability according to the ability of the operators or that apply only over trivial parameters or of minor importance, and finally there would be The abhorrent ideal that would be clearly contrary to the principle of maximum logic and the principles inherent to this one, such as the absolute order, the one of legal stringency of the system, the principle of good faith, which states do the things the best you can and the real context of freedom.

One or the factors which obliges the establishment of restrictions to freedom of thought, is represented by the context of the liberty itself, or rather the true context of freedom, which establishes: the ability to operate discreetly within range of vital action, and since the range of vital action, is framed within the parameters of minimum and maximum operating, then any other context or principle which pretends to be correlative or inherent to freedom should be subject to the absolute context of this one, which includes operating limitations in defense of the vital factor, which requires a radical paradigm shift in terms of the interpretation and management of freedom is concerned, since there are very specific parameters governing the existentialist or vital factor.

The availability of absolute contexts neutralizes or subtract force to any relative contest, and for this it is also necessary to know the true context of absolute, which can be contextualized as any factor that comes from himself, and does not allow disappearance This means that in essence the only context fully absolute the one of God, which makes any other context to be only relative, or relatively absolute with respect to God, this makes that it must be seeked at all times, to maintain the highest possible harmonic correlation with God, and especially to be careful not to grant criterion completely absolute to any other factor, also given the existence of various deities, it is necessary to try to establish which is the one true God, for which it would be of great help the figure itself of the only true God as such, because if someone invokes the only one true God, it would be indeed the God of this condition to whoever this one is calling.

The figure of the one true God, represents an important endorsement that allows you to debug in a great extent, the ideals and tenets of faith, for anyone who is not a devotee of the one true God, would not be under the protection of one God, almighty, what will make a false believer or believer of a minor religious principle to those who renege on this, and truly faithful to those who express belief, but actually this is just a way to protest, saying they believed in one and true God, but do not follow the commandments of Him, then equally it results problematic.

Being clear about what would be some absolute operational contexts that are essential for better human behavior, it's easy or relatively easy, to ignore every principle that renege these, and as a synonym of major vigor of the absolute, the understanding and establishing of the best operating parameters of these: it is represented by individuals endowed with the greatest intellectuals, which in turn allows us to rule out largely ideological disorders very commonly is seen in individuals of lower intellectual, except in the case where these be guided by the order issued by the superior intellect and cases in which less quantity, the same can be originated in minor factors, but still, it is necessary to the recognition and validation of the intellectually superior.

The fact that some individuals might offer evidence of parameters of absolute type on the operation of the system, do not make them automatically of major intellectual level, nor ruler of the system as it is typical that some of these parameters are presented in a fortuitous manner, where it is not required extra effort or intellectual work to highlight it, but still, those with the lowest intellectual level and succeed in offering parameters of absolute type, are supported by merits of lucky individual among others.

LEGALITY, LEGITIMACY AND VALIDITY

It is inevitable that the system should be governed by an established order, this as synonymous of survival and harmonious correlation between individuals, and to go without this principle, it means falling into parameters of cannibalism, but the principle of established order itself, does not guarantee survival, at least in the way that it has been handling from always, as for the context of order itself, sometimes has little to do with such a context, so sometimes it would apply better the context of prevailing status, since the context of status could refer either to an atmosphere of order or of disorder, in any case: it is preferred only an environment of strict order, preferably of absolute type, where the context of order as that of absolute are clearly defined, and from there, direct the operation of the system on this basis.

The context of order is provided by the legal rigor of the system, and is defined by the harmony as much as by the possible chaos resulting from the correlation of different basic operational factors such as the behavior of matter at a physical and chemical level, and the behavior of organic factors that regulate the human body, from this you can establish that if there is no order, then there is chaos, and if there is chaos then there is inertia and or death. The context of absolute applies almost in the same way than the one of order, but reasoned that the context of absolute is singular, and does not admit disappearance makes the same context of order be defined by the factor absolute, and since God is the only factor absolute, then the search for the established order of absolute type should start from the guidelines that on this respect may offer God and according to the mechanisms that he himself may offer, having available for this among others, the content expressed in writing in the Bible or any other holy book such as the consideration of factors not Christians, but attached to the harsh legal system.

The operation of order requires a fundamental and basic testament, setting out the different operational parameters or order status by which it should be governed the individuals, they must be strictly adhered to the legal rigor of the system and from this compilation of legal basis of this system equally it would apply the different criteria of legality, thus, any set of legal type that does not derives from the rigorous legal system while providing the most effective possible existential factor, not only do not apply as a legal but also would be subject to the supremacy of any figure that effectively would accomplish the requirement of legality that the system contains, so that by force of this, individuals would be protected from suffering the traumas that happen at being led to obeying legal figures , of cannibal or suicidal type.

Based on the law it is established the legitimacy, which can be understood as anything that derives from the law, this means that if laws are not such, neither is it the legitimacy, as a capricious modification of laws also requires a capricious modification of legitimacy, in change the laws of nature are unique and unchanging, and there is only place left for a readjustment in the event of a failure in the original interpretation of a natural law, which would deserve such a rearrangement, but in this case, it seeks to maintain the legitimate string that applies according to the case, on the interpretation that has been going according to a new one.

Even in the case that you get to set an established order of sufficient legal rigidity, it could be created situations of disorder on the basis of the interpretation that some might give to certain laws, especially by ignoring or disregarding in a significant way some operating parameters of them, or reasoned to attacks from disordered ones, this generates interpretative parameters about what would effectively have or not legal validity, for what it is necessary that every individual seeks to have the largest flow of legal knowledge as possible, especially if its taken into consideration that the breaking of laws means no single government sanction, but also of natural form, such as cases where speed is operated incorrectly, as temperature or electricity, and also in the consumption of food or substances that detrimentally alter the organic factors.

Some natural laws may not have legal governmental validity, in this case, the prudency would be to seek granting governmental criterion as well, and for this purpose, governmental factors, should be more willing, as greater management of laws, would provide more credit to the system, and by legal and validity criterion itself: it could neutralized such attacks of disordered type, that just for the simple act of being an expanded matrix, become very strong in attack by the irregular, and even the factors of order or relative order, which also have a tendency to simply provide what appears to look like good ideas, but to compare them with the principle of legal rigor of the system, they don´t apply as such, at least in the context of maximum logic.

The expanded wrong matrices achieve a high profile because there has not existed until now, a single calibration factor, as it is the legal rigor of the system, making the quest for hegemony or supremacy in the global or sectorial system, based specifically on that, rather than simply stalling in some sectors, without more criterion than widespread acceptance for some, and it would not happen that way, or at least it should not, by the sole factor, since all parameters would coincide in a single element, which is represented by the system, and this is common to all, so this way it would be something irrational, trying to create polarization within the system, knowing that the property that gets set in terms of laws, would be an asset of all, relegating the circumstances of hegemony and supremacy, to the merits to be able to achieve in this environment through discovery and management of natural laws and inherent factors.

By these criteria are abolished the hegemonic pretensions of some disorderly factors to create a multipolar world, for the simple reason that natural laws are a single block, and almost all are complementary and absolute, so to pretend to diminish the operation of some of them means an attempt against the natural order and existentiality. Similarly, the common factor, it allows to establish the obligatory need to set a status of globalization, for the same reasons given above, because in this way would be to expanding the range of action that would allow to access through harmonic correlation, all available factors that help the operational soundness of the legal environment of the system and therefore the system itself.

The claims of disorderly sectors to create a multipolar world, are truly shameful, as for they deliberately attack typical factors of supremacy, but simultaneously for reasons of operational necessity and regularity of interoperable laws of nature, they are forced to depend on these factors with those who generate rivalry, and this can sometimes be done the most shameless way possible, as in cases where some factors that have some dominance in the oil and energy factor attacking the government of the United States of America, but simultaneously they are forced to sell oil and consume goods and services generated by this nation, and this oil factor is just one of the many factors where the need for global exchange is made mandatory, but the disordered ones would seems not have shame.

In reality, the operational reasons for many disorders, is represented by their natural condition of being shameless, dishonest, cynical, immoral, crooks, criminals, etc., And the intricacies of the system have been giving them the opportunity where they can wreak their excesses, tending to deal with only sometimes to powerful factors of strength, but apparently not very powerful factors of reason, and they say apparently because actually there are factors of reason very powerful only that it has been lacking small doses of maximum reason that complemented with the existing reasons, then you can note the magnitude of the power of these.

There is much confusion in the interpretation on contexts of polarized factor concentric factor from this we have that when we talk of a unipolar world, such reference should apply in an analogically way to the case where the environment physics, there is a particle called the monopoly and this one has the characteristic of not being complemented with another pole, then: if it is unipolar, it would be illogical to propose the existence of another pole, however, if the reference is based on a multipolar world, this would apply in base to the existence of two opposite poles, where one would be positive and the other one negative, this would lead to the conjecture in the geopolitical environment on which one would be the negative and which the positive, and in this case there would be some feasibility in the case where the disordered regimes choose to assume their condition of negative factors, but even so, said condition of disorder would be subject to the pursuit of an order where it is intended to be imposed in any case, the reality indicates that the search for a multipolar world, it is oriented to create a negative pole by the disorder.

Since from this perspective it is illogical to promote or accept the existence of a multipolar world it would be left to define the existence of a concentric world, and this does result feasible, since the concentric factor is correlated with itself, that is, it allows the existence both of one or more sites, and these at the same time would be oriented in terms of providing the greater operational soundness where it functions; of this multiplicity of parameters, some sites would be relatively unique and principals, while others would be subordinate and or autonomous As an example of this we would have the United Nations (UN) as concentric governing factor of the international order and the different countries and sub regional organizations, as multiple concentric factors and relatively subordinate of the concentric factor UN, but relatively absolute or guiding of the internal order of each one of them.

This type of scheme allows a greater operational soundness of the system and it was born from the urgent need to create a concentric factor of the UN type, which converge almost any kind of geopolitical factors. Attempting to create organisms parallel to the UN agencies, represents a repetitive attitude of overcome mistakes, and in the same way, to pretend a change of headquarters, because of some inconveniences on its location, it simply means the transfer of these same problems elsewhere, making these types of hegemonic rivalry, are only fanciful attempts to disturb the order.

Almost all the concentric factors arise from maximum logical reasoning, where the operational soundness of the environment in which they arise, is very efficient, and apart from the concentric factor as such, they are inherent to this, other factors such as location and foundation or scoop, where the location would be the place where it sets the concentric factors, and factors of foundation would be represented by the factors that set the initiatives of foundation of such concentric factors. Not always in principle the location is ideal, but once established the operational center, then you start rooting operations and logistics factors based on this, and this means that almost regardless of the concentric place, the operation ends up offering great credit to factors served, such centers that in principle were not ideal, usually are presented on an empirical or accidental way.

In contrast, when previously there is a feasibility study, and with the highest professional standard, you will get better solvency at all times. As an example of both, we can cite the pre-planned food markets of the towns and villages and modern shopping centers, in both cases we can say that if these concentric factors did not exist, the products needed to be acquired, would be scattered around throughout the urban conglomerate , this would entail having to make long journeys for each of the remote distribution units of products, with consequent loss of time and effort in carrying goods across the way, however: in a distribution center where large converge number of distributors, the products can be purchased with in less time, space and effort, this type of operation is satisfactory to both consumers and sellers.

The same criterion applies to the production center of corporate type, which have large units for collection and distribution of classified or manufactured products where raw material producers can pull up their items, it can also be specified banking services, ports and airports, terminals land transport, health centers, educational centers, media, internet, etc., in fact: there are countless concentric factors and large benefits that they provide to the people: but not everything is rosy, as for if such concentric factors do not operate with some regulations, then it can lead to vices of monopoly business, which is a disordered figure of restrictive type, but based on the principle or real context of freedom it can be established that the failure to allow concentric factors it would be attempting against freedom from minor operational parameter, and if you are permitted but not regulated, as the same it would be an attempt against freedom, but from the more operational parameter.

Once a factor acquires concentric regular operational soundness, it generates harmonic correlation links and hegemonic factors in favor of all operators direct and indirect, in this case there can be mentioned the existence somewhere in a large shopping center of certain agricultural items, where the direct operators would be who participate in the activity that takes place there, and indirect those who do not participate, but will attend prestigious criteria for being associated with that place where they live or maintain a significant correlation, all these parameters of property that are generated, they come to represent different values and heritage of moral and commercial type among others.

Also it is generated competition parameters that can be of fair or unfair type, being the type of fair competition, when third operators try to operate in that space or concentric place with the consent of their traditional operators, especially those who have major hegemonic criteria of property, and also motivated by operational soundness that they see in this place, they seek to establish another place elsewhere where it may not be affected negatively the first one or even to create harmonious correlation links. Instead, unfair competition would be created in cases where using conspiracy factors, they seek to displace the traditional operators of the rectory and or property of the concentric place, and or they try to steal the customer.

The practice of messy monopoly-type operation, is typical of the disordered factors of the right, the one of conspiracy relay by sleight, extortion, expropriation, etc., It Is typical of the disordered factors of the left, and when they seek the greatest possible number of parameters of order and freedom, it is typical of central factors. In essence, there are only these three ideological factors, and out of there, there are many definitions that even if many try to establish them as different, they are always the same as the basic, as the same the ideological context could also be summarized in just two factors that would be the center and the extreme, consisting of the extreme left and right, this extreme factor is the cause of the evils of the system, and much of the effect it has, is by the lack of knowledge about the real ideological contexts of each factor, not only by factors of order, but by the same disorder factors.

SOME TYPES OF ATTACK

TYPICAL WAR ATTACK OR CONVENTIONAL: may be generated by political, religious, territorial disputes or any other strategic factor, etc., regular army Weapons are used, and there are some regulatory bodies of the excesses that they might commit as the Rome Statute of the Criminal International Court and the Geneva Convention, generally defined in base of availability, location and use of military equipment and combat capabilities of the military, both in quantity and quality, it could be avoided through factors of maximum logic and if this principle is not decisive, then the circumstances that apply more as cannibalism than anything else, this could be only by part of one of the factors, that which is denying the reason, but the results do not invalidate the principle of maximum logic whatever be the outcome, because this is absolute and sooner or later it ends up imposing itself.

GUERRILLA WARFARE: The operation scheme is somewhat identical to the previous one only that it involves an irregular army, acting furtively in most cases, it could be avoided by principle of order which states that governance can only be exercised by individuals gifted of the most respectable intellectually, very rarely order factors represent the irregular army, but this option is not ruled out entirely, especially if they are those who seek the establishment of an orderly regime, and is applicable when disorderly factors deny completely the use of reason or principles of maximum logic. Often messy factors have a lot of cunning, but not much intelligence; otherwise they would not be individuals who always seek violence or deception by guile.

ELECTION ATTACK: It consists in winning the vote for the lagging sectors by tricks and threats, but even if there is no such tricking or threats, the lagged factors do not apply as decisive factors in establishing the parameters of governance, because they simply don´t have the capacity or at least not have the same extent as the leader factors in intellectuality. The percentage of ordered leaders of high intellectuality, is overwhelmingly higher than those disordered of relatively equal condition, but the individuals intellectually lagged is also higher than the most intellectual individuals in a relationship that can reach 60% to 40% quantitative in favor of the lagged, causing that to admit the fact of taking as valid parameters for government decisions of electoral type, a list of simple majority, represents one of the worst mistakes of democracy or what it is supposed to be.

When disordered regimes observe that the electoral counter-attack of the order factors can be overcome by an absolute majority, then they changed the electoral rules, so that with fewer votes they overcome by a relative majority of votes where they have a majority of supporters, the number of representatives than the factors of order, and indeed a scheme something like it represents the ideal solution of maximum logic, but this would be where the qualitative intellectual factors of higher level, and it may be on them where the criterion of governance will fall upon. it The outline of a simple majority vote, it is irrational not only in the electoral environment of governance, but also in many other sectors, where are discriminated the qualitative factors on basis of purely quantitative factors.

ATTACK LEGALISTIC: Generated when disordered factors posses government control by a judicial monologue, and it is based on annulling almost all functionality of factors opposing its causes WITH legalistic measures, almost regardless of the irrational or shameless that they can be, they generally do this with the least scruple and trying on turn sow the largest possible course and scorn on their opponents, this is done by adhering to a strict control over public authorities, state media and private accomplices, both locally and internationally, also they trust for this: in the apparent weakening they are exercising on rival factors, with measures such as expropriation, imprisonment, exile, obstruction in permits, and other factors of state terrorism, as the same they trust in how delayed the international justice factors generally act in these cases.

The best way to counteract them would be in a preventing form, using the criteria of maximum logic containing intellectual superiority factor of government regency, however, when they are in power, they would apply measures to also get them into reason about how inconvenient it is their remain in government control, and if they do not give in, then they would apply force measures of any kind, including zero option if applicable, as long as they reach the objective of eradicating them both from the power and the possibility to exercise again. In this case, it would make sense: defeat or die rather than remain under the yoke of the disordered ones.

COMPARATIVE ATTACK: This is a typical strategy which the irregular take advantage of, with the intention to justify all their excesses and obtain impunity, this consists in linking clever and deceptively their errors with real or unreal errors committed in the past by factors of order or disorder, that would be somehow related to them, it is like trying to make it clear that nothing can blame them, because those who do so, would be factors equally guilty as them, and therefore would not have sufficient moral authority for this purpose, in essence, this is a scheme which aims to keep alive the cannibalism, leaving no room for justice factors such as innocence, forgiveness, the judged thing or penalty paid, the peace agreements, armistice, the reconciliation, the loss of effectiveness of established orders, etc.

Virtually all the factors are subject to errors committed for reasons of imperfection, which makes that according to disordered scheme, it would only be valid and feasible a set regime of cannibalism, because no one would have the moral authority to judge another, but as it turns that justice is an absolute factor, and therefore can not become obsolete, the operational scheme that they would apply in these cases is not the cannibal criterion because of imperfection, but an outline of scrutiny or average as the successes and failures of each individual, where the ones with best average in favor of the successes come to represent the Regent factors of justice, in this case it is advisable not to be fooled with a false supremacy as factors of honesty, patriotism, charisma, popularity, leadership, etc., and intelligence is only valid as an absolute factor of governance.

OPPORTUNISTIC ATTACK: Occurs when some factors are aggrieved or fall from grace, then disordered factors lend themselves to offer help, after that they seek to exercise hegemony over the factors of order, but other than that they do not meet the requirements of high intellectuality, it also seems adverse to them, the typical disordered operation of them, as they use this to generate concentric factors other than the typical operation of the order, and generate quarrels from this fact, the recommendation in these cases is that anyone who would be needing any help, do not attempt to get those aids that kill, as the would be worse the wrong than the benefits generated by the system.

In any case, anyone who is in need of help, which in the worst case, this is framed   within the so-called pragmatic opportunism, that is, that the favors are offered or received in exchange for pleas to be reprehensible and can maintained   proper principles and values. For some purposes this principle is no less reprehensible, but the same it´s attended by operational parameters that locate it within the margin of tolerance.

Equally it is generated, when some factors fall into disrepair and then the disordered ones try to take the hegemonic place of these ones, or create other ones different or parallel, this type of perverse operation is typical not only of the geopolitical environment, but also of the trivial environments, and sometimes there is no reason for help, but of divestment and misappropriation of the factors involved, common in cases of natural disasters, fires, rollovers of freight transport, urban riots, economic crisis or depression of any individual, innocence of minors etc. Sometimes disasters are not random, but actually are generated by the same disordered ones.

Opportunistic attacks are also generated in routine situations, such as cases of the correlation, employer- employee, collector –payer-debtor, ruler-citizen marriage relationship, offer - demand, etc., in them it is played much arrogance, morbidity, the clever scam, and the trickeries, and are based on a development within the boundaries of legal and illegal, where seeking a legal solution could be more traumatic than the relative value of interpretive factor in this role, which almost always is money, or the same way, trying an illegal way out, asthe same it would have worse consequences for the punitive effect of the laws, the morbidity of this is generated when acting in bad faith, or put it in another way: when you lack the principle of good faith, or to do things the best way possible.

Also the operations develope within a discretionary operational band or tolerance, which the legal system leaves to the discretion of the operators, because it exercises legal routine operation in it, it would supersaturate justice mechanisms because of the so abundant that such cases would be, even so there are some judicial figures as Judge of the Peace, which usually attend these minor operations, also can be seen by the ordinary justice, but the economic costs sometimes makes them inconvenient for all or almost all of the operators, especially because of the judicial inflation figure: procedural costs and charges for damage and injury in such cases justice acts paradoxically inflating the absolute value of the thing, to give priority to a relative high value on this.

Not always who collects a debt, does it so arrogant, but sometimes, especially when there is some delay in the implementation of this, indeed they act with great pride, sometimes making the situation surrounded by much morbidity, and this of course generally creates trauma to the debtor, in these cases: if for the debtor would be impossible to fulfill that commitment he would not be acting in bad faith, but would be subject to circumstances, but when the debtor can meet the commitment to pay, and it does not, then indeed there would be bad faith, especially when the debt becomes knowing beforehand that this could not pay, and sometimes he who should meet payment commitments, would not necessarily be a weak or relatively weak factor in favor of a strong or relatively strong factor, but that the commitments might actually be a strong factor in favor of a weak one, as the case of the correlation between employers and employees.

These patterns may be both state and private factors, and bad faith is generated almost always, when providing resources for the payment, we prefer to retain this money earning interest in banks or other commercial factor, generating a typical trauma employees lack of resources that are routinely required to obtain at times become necessary on the part of employees, type of counter strike, protest, strike, etc. in order to force payment of their wages withheld, this operation also is generated when After payment of debts, are necessary wage adjustment are claims or other claims, but employees are not always the victims, but sometimes, often in collusion with union leaders, employers attack, using the same figures strikes, protests or strikes, calling claims that the employer can not comply, or if true, would be through debt measures traumatic or subtracting operational possibilities in other sectors, generating from one side and an atmosphere of cannibalism.

Opportunistic attacks are usually done discreetly and poaching, and by one or a few individuals, but in other cases, are performed in the presence of some groups, which can range from just two individuals, to the audience that may have an address on national television media by a head of state, in these cases, there is seldom economic interest, at least directly, because the targets are almost always designed to generate the weak factor, a disgrace, and in some cases victims are not aware that the scorn and derision that would be subject, or if you would, but for reasons of need or guilt, accept the ignominious exposure to situations in these cases, the attackers act covered by arrogance of the strong towards the weak, trying to enjoy the trash as it produces perverse.

In some arts, this type of operation has been professionalized collegial or quite some time, but is conducted within the parameters of a tolerance, which may even be covered by criteria of maximum logic, but also can be highly reprehensible not in its default form, but its content parameters in cases where in fact the operation is beyond the tolerance as an example of this we can cite the figure of satire, and parody, which can be exposed by many expressive means, the most entrenched the cartoons, literature, music and theater, they can be a factor both in attack and counterattack, and can be filled with satisfaction to the correlation attacker or just one, and third factors or spectator and aware public.

Satire seeks the promotion of personal convenience factors, using specious resources, subliminal, or side of a particular variable type, which would strengthen a cause or self-rooted, innovative or just incidental, using the tolerance that would involve a Discrete factor kind of clandestine or semi-clandestine, where the underground is not necessarily seeking to evade the legal order, but to a factor reprehensible by some allied sectors, adverse or neutral, or equally may be a correlation of factors which seeks allies win favor or indulgence, and an adverse factor which generally seeks some defeatism, there are some parameters which seeks a rapprochement with an enemy or objectionable factor, ignoring relatively, how bad could be seen that such an attitude by a factor ally in this case seeks to dismiss the figure of betrayal, the figure for the council.

The parody is almost always used in correlation with the satire, one can even say that both inherent, and it seeks to recreate some real faces through the dramatization, often using extreme of this trend as the lyric, but taking immediate objective satirical give context to what is expressed, and say that the ultimate objective, to achieve some political purpose may be religious, social, economic, racial, national, and the most dissimilar motives. The economic factor and the entertainment, do not always act as the final objective of satire, but as inherent goals, and this is in cases where the playwrights and authors of satire perceived economic benefits, regardless of ultimate goal and also when the target the end is mere entertainment, dismissing the side reaches the reasons that might have satirical, and even if these come to be significant.

Sometimes it is extremely difficult to sort out which would be the margins of toleration that might have some facts or events that are promoted as satire, this event is generating in its turn, a major concern by factors that could be affected significantly by this, such as some political, religious, economic, social, etc., and sometimes trying to guard against this potential adverse choose to restrict the media satire or operational practice, mainly the media and attacks on producers, writers, actors, satirists factors as media owners, and also lash out at almost any other factor may arise situations where opportunistic attack by the tolerance that should be satire.

This type of means is highly pernicious, because the satire as such, it contains parameters that provide maximum operational logic of absolute type, as seeking a ban or eradication: it is a traumatic event that threatens the true beginning of freedom, in this way, just try to debug it operating parameters which would evade the margin of tolerance, but not tolerance as such, not only against the satire, but against the tolerance that the same should have any factor operating maximum logic both as minor, these being less logic, more complicated and that, therefore, would need further refinement.

Satire is a factor that historically has been immersed in parameters of stigma, which fortunately have been lost force, were so traumatic, it involves both the attackers and counter-attacking factors, such as collateral factors, as an example of them, we would to the factors of racial rivalry and filmmakers side of satire, which may or may not directly part of the rivalry, in these cases, the attack parameters are generated based on stigma of racial prejudice, by a certain race that for a given time history is taken by fine, by some factors that maintained economic supremacy, government, military, social etc., and oppressed racial factors accounted weak, and generally were of low economic, social, military, government and culture.

Stigmatic consequences of prejudice remained in force even beyond the requested lifetime of the established order of a governmental nature, but these were becoming outdated as well pushed by some sectors of the once exquisite factors, which preferred to leave the class in an attempt to attack harmonic correlation, and sometimes, they were forced to face by force factors to sectors engaged in hegemonic subjugation, in many cases forming common cause with the factors under despotic rule, apart from the growth in factor accumulation and hegemonic of these, which then was widely equated with the above factors in conflict.

Many of these stigmata persisted to a lesser extent until recent, and even very low level, still has some validity, although it has also noticed that left such factors have been seeking some false claims about events of the past relatively neglected, generating stigmatic parameters of reverse bias to the above, where now the once-weak sectors, discriminate against equally strong factors once, and it is that the former are far weaker, but reasoned criteria of false logic, manage to be corralled under the guidelines totally illogical absurdities of parameters of the democratic ideal, which lend themselves to keep alive, but obviously, this happens because they have not noticed even with sufficient clarity, the illogic of the case, especially as it relates to echo where a majority of lower intelligentsia, is the ruler of the order on the most intellectual individuals, and this affects cough sectors regardless of the role that their ancestors occupied.

The stigmas generated were so large that the oppressive and segregated settings, operating across the board on nearly all factors pertaining to a particular race or socioeconomic status, so that such individuals being white segregated the blacks, as foisted upon them derogatory parameters of almost all types, such as criminals, and this because apart from just being in the race then marginalized, many of these individuals in their courses, they were forced to criminal conduct, as was the case with those of low socioeconomic level, where by simply being poor and had them all for criminals, taking in many bullrings these individuals, to appeal to leniency parameters, where factors clarified them or caring for them, which in the case of blacks, were black but white soul, on the case of the poor, who were poor but honest. The soul refers to the color white that allegorically represents the soul, not a similarity with the white race.

Ignominious parameters of satire, not only on factors may fall under the attacks of this, but sometimes also affects the makers of satire, especially the actors, but in these cases the characters almost always act in an attempt to obtain any economic benefit through money left by fans at the box office this trend, or through payment received from media producers or theater, in these cases the actor himself is the target, exposing themselves to situations that trigger a sense of humor, with purely artistic grounds, or sometimes simple joke, but sometimes this kind of ridicule as it has more artistic content of mockery as such and say that the margin of tolerance, is framed within the ignominy that could exposed to derision prove under certain parameters, or the care taken in ensuring that all this framed within the merely artistic, yet based on the how complicated it is to establish what would be the parameter of tolerance, could generate different target those who want to get, especially if what is sought is only economic benefits.

One of the factors that most often find it difficult to escape the ignominy parameters, represents the legendary figure of the clown, because no matter how refined the role art can be sometimes represent: for some individuals, a clown is nothing than a burlesque character condition, this idiosyncrasy also affects other actors than the clown humor, in this case it would be regrettable, the lack of wisdom that allows to correctly work and noble that may exist in a satirical performance when actually have healthy and professional approach, and also by the attack that he would be doing the healthy sense of humor of the citizens, because this healthy sense of humor is a natural condition of the individual who begins to glimpse even from the first moments of life or newborn stage.

The ignominy as a business, a factor widely exploited, and is sometimes used as a springboard to some parameters of supremacy in some sectors, such as the entertainment and politics, both in individual cases where the character acting is the focus of shame, as when this is addressed to third parties within the characters in the show business environment may include artists of all genres, singers and musicians in general, modeling figures, etc., as may be included among these, the socially relevant figures, sometimes called solcialité, and sports figures, and in this environment to almost any figure of the show, in the political environment can be singled out to leaders subject to popular election and those who favor measures of facto like the so-called revolutionaries and the coup.

In the atmosphere of the show is common for overflow parameters where the margin of tolerance, disordered factors do generate extravagance, scandal, ridicule, cynicism, scorn, lust, etc., And between these characters and the fans or followers of them, generated an atmosphere of general morbidity and morbidity is precisely the main attraction of the matter, which drags the integrity smaller individuals, usually young people and adults from low culture, but within the business makers and a few other critics, are individuals of relatively high culture, but little honor, which aims to make money on an opportunistic basis, relying on the exploitation of what has come to be handled as reprehensible, and indeed it is, or not, but still maintains a high level of confidence about it.

When factors are unquestionably reprehensible, what actually committed a crime or social sacrilege, but in the legal government, sometimes there is no greater motivation to strive for eradication, control or censorship, because it could lead to a loss of political support leaders, creating an atmosphere of complicity between the promoters of the show and fan voters, which in turn causes an increase in the global environment degenerative spiral, but this bargain for the use or exploitation of ignominy, represents an opportunity not to let the leaders losing political cynicism, and sometimes they try to be the protagonists of morbidity or co-stars with the factors of the show, in this case the counter-attack situations look more difficult, as the leadership tries to surround himself with impunity cynical monopolizing the control of regulatory factors and doers of justice.

In the context of morbid fans, this hobby is not necessarily generated through the atmosphere of the show, but through personal interaction environment, and may be through temptation or seduction, or by forcible compulsion, this latter is widely used by factors linked to drug trafficking, the pimps, the political and religious cynicism, in these cases, attempts to break the dignity of the individual, by threats, or immersed in high standards of shame, so that once collapsed psychologically, they choose to surrender the designs of their tormentors, something very similar to the operation occurred in the so-called Stockholm syndrome.

Among the methods used may be mentioned a large personal political activism by individuals indoctrinated for these purposes, a large deployment of semantic factors as clothing allegorical attack their causes, the use of red by left-wing extremists , the most representative, usually accompanied by high concentrations of followers, and all that is provided to a montage of miracles and lying wonders.

Government's attack factor, using extortion and blackmail, subtracting or offering them job opportunities on condition of political support to this economic largesse are added as a factor in purchase of conscience, which some of those who give, but by acting circumstances than by conviction, but the vast majority are bargain hunters operating under the gross array rosy star or serve as a luxurious extras to drift towards the leader of idolatry and the cause, yet, unfortunately for these individuals, seemed like a good opportunity at first, then transforms into a severe trauma, because the factors of greater capacity, operating parameters prefer to withdraw to where there is no more or no correlation with the disordered regime, apart from the endeavor of the disordered system to lash out against them, resulting in the generation of a socio-economic chaos, where inflation and actual unemployment, reaching record levels, the pair to be restricting the freedom of all factors.

Attacks exploiting the ignominy carried out by the main leader is usually around their peers in ignominious followers, is aimed at both competing factors, as himself, abound in them exceeded parameters of offenses of all kinds, trying to discredit to the maximum, whatever seems the enemy, both locally and globally, it almost never misses the eschatological language or

54

commonly own situations are ridiculous, but this attitude is digested by the masses happy follower, just has a habit of breaking almost all parameters of the protocol, and most of this is framed in a cynical media show, the most of the time on national television media.

As for the idols of the show, shameful attacks, also are intended to exceed the tolerance, and at the same time to satisfy the morbid appetite of lovers of ignominy, and see that abound this class of individuals, as economically represent a significant segment of the market, so much so that the makers of the traffic of shame, usually occupy the top places in the ranking of those who earn more money each year, I of the richest, which is also the symbol of admiration by individuals gross matrix, ie: those not purged between good and evil, but in the case of money for example, support the achievement of this without charge as obtained.

In general, the exploitation of shame is not just acting out of tolerance, but to ensure that such parameters as exhausted, they become part of the established order, which would be something like the reissue of the pre-Flood world or of the region of Sodom and Gomorrah but fortunately, in today's world there are enough people in order to prevent the whole range of parameters or destruction exceeds the percentage allowed, which cause destructive indignation and wrath of God as occurred at the world and communities mentioned above, where only the righteous Noah and the Flood pre event, the righteous Lot and his relatives through them both, were the only ones to be saved from destructive punishment, for these purposes also seeks existence of a world with some degree of tolerance, but seeks the total eradication of all forms of destruction, but if they persist even sectors of the

destruction, this would not be a defeat for the whole, but only for the lost ,
and a triumph for the areas of order.

Within specific parameters that exceed the tolerance in the world of
entertainment, would include:

A - MUSIC: Lyrics containing sex without limits, rhythms and dances of
highly lewd and lascivious content, that have high contended some explicit
sex.

B - FILM AND THE LIKE, as in music, but contents are quite explicit morbid
attack and aberrant in the case of porn, and while it does not happen the
same way television or theater, seeks to strongly penetrate and convert these
sectors in fields of the same ilk as the porn film.

C - MODELING: In this case, something that seems or should look like the
art of dressing people and especially women, seem rather the art of
undressing and leave them naked or with just a washcloth or device that leave
the impression that there was some ingenious design or fashion, and for
those involved in attacks such morbid, almost no matter how much lust or
frivolous may be exposed women who like it, but all that matters would be
fashionable, and hegemony and make money for promoters.

Also exploited at the extravagance of madness, as in the case of some
truly wacky designs content, where little bizarre or crazy mind of these, it
would simply be a new trend in dress, and both these cases as in the previous
the burden is shameful attempt to make it fall on those who oppose those
fads, or latest fashions, accusing them of being clad in the ancient culture,

marginal, Puritans, blessed, and so on., trying to show that who have the supremacy in dressing are those who operate within the parameters lewd fashion, the "cannon fodder" in these cases, representing both the characters engaged in modeling, and users.

D - SOCIALITE: these are figures from the world of high society call or jet set, who have little or no role in the aforementioned activities, but if a lot of correlation with those who wander in them, mainly with the most flamboyant and held, and along with them, also come to be considered a celebrity.

E - SPORTS: In this sector where exploitation of shame, usually occur by chance and they are pleased the public more than frivolous entertainment of athletes, although it is quite large the audience that likes both environments, in which sporting environment because of the very essence of sport, players and athletes should be kept under strict fitness regime very refined, to which they are counter the excesses that make the entertainment environment, but still, sometimes some comment athletes if such excesses, which in reality is accused by the bulk of the fans, but very pleased for the tabloids and the followers of this, the disgraceful situations arise from the time when cases are uncovered some excesses they are committed illegal and scandalous situations arise, managers in naming names and exposing the excesses of sports celebrities, like those of almost any other environment, often occur through stealthy cameramen and photographers, commonly known as paparazzi.

While the ignominy traffickers represent a sector subject to criticisms by factors of order, this does not discourage them in their pursuit of profit, since in addition they have the consent of messy sector, profit is almost always significant , and precisely because of bad fame or infamy, represent one of the biggest factors that are worth promoting, holding almost always at the maximum which reads: No matter who speak ill of you, what matters is to talk, which is very similar to the maxim that leaders make use of political cynicism that says: the end justifies the means, and while a good purpose can be achieved by good means, the extremists are worth is despicable means to ensure the end of the same nature, or even if the order seems noble, this is undermined by the execrable of the means used to achieve this.

ATTACK "ANTI-IMPERIALISM", is generated by ignorance or manipulation context of what applied in a time like imperial realm, and what applied then and now as a great and powerful nation, of this we usually large and powerful nations of antiquity also were imperial realms, what originated that homogeneity or merger of contexts, but is that not all imperial realm was a great and powerful nation or any nation great and powerful kingdom was an imperial, though generally these if they were, and this factor is what led most of which are alike in both contexts, we have this when speaking of a great and powerful nation is indeed so, but when speaking of empire, there is much ambiguity as it in essence imperial government, is one who rules with empire, that is: so imperative, therefore subduing their own people and foreign nations, which was very common to do so under slavery. Part of the confusion is also due to the underside of the term spread imperativism that best applies to your context root, spread was that of imperialism.

But at least now, the big and powerful nations do not rule on a mandatory, and in this case might have to exclude China, by reason the mandatory scheme which has left-wing and the newly defunct Soviet Union. In the Soviet case, the pleas of fact can be established that apart from great and powerful nation, was also an imperial or imperialist nation, and as the hegemonic center of the empire, acting Russian Federal Republic, which had under regency or domain imperative not only other nations that made up the Soviet Union, but also several eastern European nations, united in what became known as the Soviet bloc or the Iron Curtain, in addition to great influence in other countries located in Asia, Africa and Cuba in Latin America, nations whose regimes these inmates were or are exercised in turn so imperative, which states that it is not necessary that a great and powerful nation is to apply as imperialist rulers.

In the case of the United States of America, this is a great and powerful nation, but it is extremely paradoxical, describe it as imperialist, as the contrary is the nation where the most parameters set to the true context of liberty, internally and with other countries, and more paradoxical and ironic is the fact, that very few if by imperialist regimes like Cuba, whoever they are bent over it, this echo is a clear example of fascism, or to foist on others to have the defects that have not really, but the same prosecutor has them can be said that failures in freedom seen in the United States, are due to that they don't yet handle the real context of freedom.

The problem is not just words or concepts, but on lateness since most of the operation of the factors imperial past, it has lost relevance, in an almost total and almost said, precisely because those who attack in the present factors that branded as imperialist, it is they who try to reissue these old and detestable practices, using fascist methods and perspectives on subliminal, but carefully analyzed, the contents are very obvious fascist, these promoters also neo imperialism, seeking parameters of domination by traitors in the service of a foreign power, or traitors factors as best they are known, they can cover up even the president of a nation's military leaders, heads of public authorities and a wide popular network support, mainly as a sleeping, Network which was originally exhibited as mere supporters of ideals and or leaders of the foreign power which then would exercise imperial control.

CRUEL CAPITALISM: the principle of capitalism, represents a fundamental and basic operating factor in the context of state and government, making it also represents a basic factor of all ideological principle, even if it seeks to deny it, this echo turn left to expose the fallacy of the claims of leftist ideals, not just try to ignore capitalism, but even attack him, because capitalism, represents only the economic wing of the productive management of every nation, and although a sometimes speak of state capitalism as the only valid or necessary factor in the end after all this talk about the validity of capitalism as such, only when the state that has a monopoly of capital is simply subtracting the operational capacity any measure that can provide the private sector, which represents a serious violation of the true context of freedom.

Usually we speak of capitalism as a factor belonging only to the ideal of democracy and the center or right ideal, and sometimes it is confused as an ideological factor apart with its own operation, but it is also fallacious, because as mentioned above Capitalism is just the economic wing of any political ideal, and since the context of policy or political element is interpreted as simply the complement of the religious element makes the capitalism principle also applies to the religious element, but with the essence of each one of them.

Can not live without working capital, let alone after the invention of money, and although it survived in primitive times based on fishing, hunting and gathering of plants, it was because there was simply no alternative known same applies to the operation of barter, and although the latter still allows some valid operation, the parameters are very limited where feasible, especially in relation to operational supremacy represents money, as an example: say that is not the same the ease with which they can carry a certain amount of cash or electronic, that have to go around lugging heavy loads of goods to transact business in this limiting case it would eventually not only the heavy and cumbersome for some loads but sometimes these are perishable, and losses generated by that fact, among many other problems.

We can say that in the primitive world, capital was represented by the effort that was available and needed to ensure consumer goods, from hunting, fishing and gathering, and the availability of consumer goods provided incidental, this the same way as at present, the capital of the vast majority of the population is represented in the efforts made by working to ensure the interoperable money factor, that allows access to the purchase of consumer goods , and reasoned that can sometimes elaborate both the availability of money and consumer goods, and in others it may dwindle severely, that due to factors including weather, plagues, wars, soil quality, etc., Man considered that the most logical, was seeking to accumulate capital, either in money, as represented in all kinds of consumer goods and shelter, and infrastructure and support mechanisms for both purposes, and so far we can say that everything looked very nice .

But then came operational services as a product of greed, jealousy, resentment, and the circumstances that led to the monopoly and hoarding parameters, thereby decreasing the operational possibilities to others and some types of dependence generated hegemonic situations also generated plots against factors most solvents and these factors against the less creditworthy, equally hegemonic purposes, and from here we can say that hatred begins factors left against the capital and capitalism, and the expansion of the same leftist, and say that the tragic part of this, it represents the echo that leftists, dedicated to fighting back from the vices of capitalism, was devoted to fighting capitalism itself, with all the tragedies that this sequel has shown.

This attack and oppose capitalism, has represented a kind of "hot potato in your mouth" to leftists, by reason of the fact that capitalism is a fundamental and indispensable factor for operating any ideological factor, whatever it is called, and seeking solve this operational failure, given for promoting the "state capitalism", which is valid only as a contingency factor, temporary, small scale, but in any case as monopoly capital management by the state, mainly because the state needs the human factor to be governed, making the human factor that drives the state monopoly in a leftist regime in what capitalists call cruel, cruel capitalism and the practice of this type of operation.

62

State capitalism does not exist as such, since this is just a way of referring to the term capitalism across the state, and from the human factor that may have the different parameters of capitalism to drive, and even if the capital apparently not form part of the state, as paradoxically leftist factors have arisen, even so: it can still be used the term state capitalism, but with the caveat that this is a form on call throughout the state capitalism, that capitalism state has two operational aspects, which are: a) - the statist, the state run by cruel capitalists, in which exercise a complete monopoly or near-total capital management across the state, b) - the private: the state capitalism that operates in a free market environment, and operates only as a contingency, temporary and very small scale, particularly in cases where the private sector does not have enough capital to operate, or where bailout when generating economic crisis, trying at all times to privatize or re-privatize the capital, is also operating in case of subsidies and incentives.

The criteria of cruelty do not apply to mere fact of monopoly capital, but also the way they try and exercise, which is carried out with little regard for the least tragic cost in human lives and losses of all types they generate, especially economic and moral in this item are also included right-wing extremists, and we can say that the biggest difference between them is that right-wing extremists operating cruelly when slavery was part of the established order, and Instead left-wing extremists do not use legal parameters of slavery relatively as in the past, but use what is known as call or neo-slavery, and this case does not require individuals to work, but use of the need for their work for submission to their will, paying them meager income, subjecting them to a highly restricted consumption rate, and restrictions on freedom in large scale, and to make matters worse, as a measure of gratitude and satisfaction with the regime and their leaders, such individuals are compelled to express unconditional support to them.

Aside from the cruel capitalism, some factors right and center, also practice what some call the savage capitalism, the usually applied on large corporations, and through this practice is sought benefits on conventional operating margins, through such holes ignored by the legal regulations, or much it intends to establish a regulation would outweigh the inconvenience caused to children capitalist factors, this does give the impression that unbridled capitalism has been supported against the small, but it's all Otherwise, there is as a protectionist measure to small capitals.

But where culpable if operating parameters of savage capitalism, is in cases of indiscriminate exploitation of natural resources, especially non-renewable, and in contrast to remedy this and on average, there was what some called sustainable development or self-sustained, which includes meeting the present needs without compromising future options.

In fact it applies more savage capitalism as a case of bad reputation than anything else, even when the operation reaches wild seems critical parameters of discomfort to other factors, this chooses to withdraw and just down to the level of conventional capitalism, also has the inconvenience that is sometimes confused with parameters apply as capitalism is cruel.

Savage capitalism practiced by factors of center and right, but not left, they promote the phobia against capitalism itself, however cruel capitalism is practiced by extremists factors both right and left, and they do it because have no limitations in the environment of order, have the capitalist center. And in the case of leftism, the cruel practice of capitalism, so poaching is not so much by the aberrations that comment, but also very sneaky handling of the practice of capitalism, but obviously, just enough to find out some realities, so it does not actually have doubts, not only are capitalists, but capitalists are essentially cruel.

The ideological dissimulation apply not only on the operation to be performed, but also on quality of life of national leaders to this end we will say that it is public knowledge, taste factors that show the center and right on a life of luxury , and is also public knowledge, the vicious attack opposition leftists, the factors against such forms of life, towards the ultimate of ironies, it is also common knowledge that the echo left government leaders also live in identity parameters of quality of life than the center and right, for these as well as previous, live in luxurious homes, warehouses are transported in comfortable land, air and marine safety have spectacular rings, eat, drink and smoke so exquisite dress from top designers, look the best watches, etc.

This also reveals what appears to be true love, I envy you leftist leaders to enjoy the sweetness of luxury and comfort at the expense of vile deception carried out not only on their marginal followers, whom he exhorts content with only a "pittance" and then be forced to say that the revolution has given them all, but their rivals center, that somehow or otherwise accept the ideological force of aberrant left ideal, especially when permit through an election, are factors behind intellectually who decide what would be the ruling ideology, disregarding even the supremacy of intellectual leadership.

Another standard errors of capitalism or free market, is generated because there are no limits to allow a separate operation, including conventional investments and investment risk, that occasionally causes because of their own context, investments risk or high risk, collapsing because they can not support themselves, and generate an economic bubble that usually explodes, bringing with conventional investments, and generating widespread economic chaos, which can be avoided by just keeping a separate operation between the different investment so that the collapse of the bubble at high risk, does not affect or minimize impact on the standard investment usually is fiercely self-sustaining.

In this aspect of the collapse of financial bubbles of capitalism have long theorized leftist ideologues, but back to seek solution to the problem of the bubble, considered that the solution lay in the eradication of capitalism itself, and this fact coupled with the cruel capitalism of the right factors, it has served the left to get the great effect that had at one time and that somehow or other still remain, but as we have seen: the real goal was to emulate the practices left the cruel capitalism of the right wing, and therefore to eradicate or settle such factors as the center, and in this case the spoils looked and still looks very significant, not only provides for the control of the state capital and assets, but also the confiscation , nationalization and control of private capital in many cases owners running through subterfuge aberrant shysters of Courts.

Motivated to the relative loss of life of these people's courts and the confiscation without giving back to the owners the value of seized assets and their eventual compensation, now cruel capitalists of leftism, it is worth kidnapped courts subject to the will of them, which in some way or another makes them keep the same legal framework and operational relatively popular tribunals of the past, and also try to offer any compensation for seized property, which never actually paid or pay less than the real value and almost always make it very late, this pack of dispossession, it is usually reinforced with parameters cruel form of capitalism posed by drug trafficking, in this case, the parameters of cruelty are generated from the severe damage it causes individual consumption of these substances, mainly young people, so sometimes widespread violence unleashed and the damage they do to the economy of the countries, through the practice known as money laundering.

The experience has lived in the People's Republic of China, is a clear example of how both can coexist leftism as capitalism, and not only that, it is also fully demonstrated the supremacy of capitalism as an economic factor in the context of governance, As is true of Russia and all countries framed within the former iron curtain, only the Russians, apart from the practice of free market capitalism, also preferred the option of maximum equal logic, to establish a democratic or centrist, that also should be the next step in China because of free market capitalism is insufficient, if at the same time restrict personal freedoms, or put another way: if at the same time maintain parameters of cruelty against citizens.

In the case of Cuba, is also being implemented means of promoting private capitalism, which, in principle, some 500,000 public employees would be fired to test supplied in the private sector, and also because the state can no longer sustain the immense bureaucracy and degenerative generated by the statist capital. In this case, along with China and Eastern Europe, citizens of these countries had to be subjected to more severe trauma, seeking to oppose the greatest resistance possible to the validity of almost any parameter of private capitalism, for further as we have seen, at last, successfully entered reason, understanding that the only way to guarantee the greatest satisfactions for the citizen, the free-market capitalism, and to seek to impose at all costs, the effect of the almost obsolete all parameters, leftist ideal.

The ideal regime occurs only if the ideological context is center, which includes a free market economy, and privatizing type, otherwise there will always be traumas: for example in the case of China with a leftist government system and economy free market, the trend is that sooner or later, one devours the other two factors, namely: o finally China adopts a system of central government, otherwise, have no alternative but to return to the obsolete system of capitalism demonstrably statist or cruel, and this is because both factors of left and private capitalism are incompatible, this makes what is currently living in China, is but the preamble to the establishment of a central system or the economic collapse to the droop again.

In this case we want is the triumph of wisdom and humility and try to eradicate every vestige of pride as they did the East Europeans and begins to apply to Cuba, and as we made them the rulers of China, to remove the commends statist capitalism and establish a capitalist economy privatizing, levels of citizen satisfaction and prestige that has been reaching China, represents an excellent promotional offer for it, also the contributions that have been doing international capital, but as long as there a regimen left, the tendency of these, would be to withdraw, pending a review on the form of government.

This strategic withdrawal, is both by choice and convenience forced, for those who somehow made trade with China, outside of what might be called the margin of tolerance parameters are at risk of rejection by other factors capitalist to renege on the Chinese leftist regime, in this environment the most notable so far has been some cases of rejection of the internet environment operators, which have somehow acted in apparent complicity with the Chinese government, submitting to censorship Internet access to citizens of that nation, but this would be only a warning or preamble to what could then be a situation of such widespread, affecting almost all sectors and factors. China is also experiencing strong criticisms and pressure from some governments, by having an undervalued currency, which favors exports in an unfair, damaging the global economy.

The spectacular economic growth rate annual interest China has been experiencing, and begins to slow, and this is another clear warning of how inconvenient it is, try to keep afloat an economy where the survival of a leftist regime type, with a Capitalist economy Private type. China's situation is a case of forced digitizing where: o establishing a centrist rate regime to safeguard the economy, or else they would be inexorable return to the abyss of economic turmoil; it just forced them to changing economy statist capital by privatizing economy.

Another aspect that is affecting the Chinese capitalism is represented by the low quality of many manufactured products, but in this case have already been starting to implement corrective measures, but still get a very satisfactory level of quality looks utopian or impossible, as the leftist and quality are enemies, and it is extremely difficult for an individual who possesses an excellent concept of quality is also a leftist, or put another way: it is unlikely that a leftist has a great concept of quality, as required by global capitalism.

Besides this, much of China's economic boom is based on the mass production of low-cost goods, framed within the parameters of low wages and low commodity prices and currency undervalued, and improving the quality: it is necessary to acquire more expensive raw materials, and pay higher wages, in a directly proportional relationship where higher quality, higher cost of wages and supplies, and inverse proportion, where higher quality, lower sales on account of higher prices, on par with the reduced sales, also reduces employment.

To conclude we can say that, to compete with high quality products, represents a major challenge for the Chinese, because this market segment is largely dominated by countries that traditionally have operated under a democratic government and free commends market. All this means that China would have to compete in a difficult penetration, sacrificing a large market presence easily penetrable as it has shown so far, producing and selling merchandise at very low price. The fact that implementing a system of democratic government, help machismo, but even so, would the brake that is having a huge population, in need of jobs, job security, and improvements in income. In any case the most logical and China seeks to effectively increase the quality without sacrificing the existential factor.

COUNTER MEASURES

Motivated much of the functionality of the ideological war is the result of misunderstandings and fallacies context, also makes much of the operation needed to end this war would unravel unequivocally, these entanglements contextual, or at least in what is considered, would be the logical maximum parameters that apply to each factor, this would allow sensible citizens, be equipped with the best tools that lead to a harmonious environment correlation. Can also be said that has always sought the desired peace, it is worth saying that is very much what has been achieved, but clearly there are still some kinks, but that would not be many, as evident is that still generate large trauma different magnitudes in all sectors.

Hegemonic conflicts usually arise from the lack of what is known as evidence, which is typical of the judicial environment, and indeed, the judicial environment, the ideological and social gatherings of the different criteria of dialectics, have much in common, and could even be said that all pursue a common goal, but generally say that they all represent sequences of science, only that some actually are analyzed under the scientific rigor, while others, not at all come to scientific rigor, or any approach to this, but that does not detract from actually represent a sequence of science, this factor because of its very nature, generates irrefutable parameters, especially when it uses mathematics, but the actual mathematics are always present in the science, directly or indirectly.

Within the sequence is also scientific experimental phase, but the experimental factor not always operate under scientific rigor to this effect:

say it may even be part of the daily operations of the human being, which is like saying that everything occurs or is it experimental approach, these experimental parameters, therefore, apply equally to government operation and therefore, the economy and capitalism, and on this basis we can say that it is a serious strategic mistake: if given the importance of the governance, operational and decision-making, not made with the highest scientific rigor, especially the most important, as the form of government itself and most of its parameters, and actually commit this grave error is something that happens even daily.

This provides great potential for opportunistic attacks on working swindlers of all kinds, including political cynicism, that people had no ability to compete against operators with the highest scientific rigor, try entangle the environment or make use of the existing clutter, to generate the trauma that has, in many cases at the cost of the death of thousands or millions of human beings, moral and material losses and incalculable and irreparable. In the scientific environment, the most logical is that once established a theory and then proceed to an investigation by a small sample that is representative of a universal type to investigate, and that the conclusions of the investigation or evidence arising from case, it will expand the pilot stage to a growing universe, according to the solvency or viability of the conclusions drawn.

This operation can be implemented the criteria of the initial theory in the case that the evidence is shown to be feasible, or can discard the original theory criteria if they are discovered evidence indicating some substantial drawbacks. But it is clear that the vast majority of political operatives, are rarely guided by scientific rigor, and implement plans based on what appears

72

to be the absolute or relative majority opinion of some operators, bringing the trauma resulting lack of precision can generate, and the magnitude of such traumas are generated as the imperfections or sometimes existent aberrations, both in political ideals, and in general operation. Sometimes decisions are made effectively on the basis of scientific rigor, but this almost always occurs for the singular cases of scientific operation, but not generic operation.

The science factor yields an unique and irrefutable, not the fuzzy factors, which may yield countless results in some cases, a sample of this can be seen in some internet forums, which seek to impose our own criteria rather than criteria unique, even sometimes in the search for a single purpose, in these cases: to the dialectic itself out of sight, but not the gathering, whose sole purpose seems to be devoted to spend time and perhaps reaffirm the personalities and behaviors, even so, domestic destinations, end up being defined by the gathering, but not because of compelling reasons, but for the chance of a majority in an election result as a paramount factor of reason or personal convenience, which like it or not , being this a messy factor, sooner or later degenerate, which is not the case when decisions are made based on the criteria of maximum logic thrown by science.

However, if one side is set to be operating scientific rigor, and another based on fuzzy factors, it may be imposed degenerating factors to diffuse scientific factors, or these debugging a fuzzy factors, and obviously more would be logical for global operation is finally shaped by scientific rigor, and sometimes actually pro scientific factors are those imposed in most general election, and this is what has allowed the major benchmarks of progress in developed countries and developing, but the selective operation is based on the most general factor, and such is the established order, but not scientifically rigorous, therefore, the most logical is that the established order, apply only to government's choice and selectivity based on scientific rigor.

In this aspect it is good to keep in mind that the operation carried out by humans, not always is mainly based on reason, but sometimes is more fundamental one operation motivated by other factors such as hunger I ambition, mainly power and wealth, and these factors has much power of deception at the level of leaders and followers, so much so, that the school of dialectical practice is focused on the recruitment and indoctrination of the factors behind accomplice, being easier to manipulate and to be more numerous than the efficient intellect, leadership and socio-economic, and of course, this collection is not made clear but subliminal form, but even so, on the evidence, which shows the complicity of some and the falsity of others.

Many of the leftist ideologues of the dialectic, argue that the human operation is a class struggle, where those with economic power are nothing to what we call cruel capitalists, and socio-economic factors behind, live or have lived in such a condition, not a product of their courses and circumstances, but for reasons of oppression, dispossession, and exclusion violated by the factors of economic leadership, and in reality they are right, because there are plenty of evidence to show that in many cases actually is, but in reality, such a dialectic, is full of lies and falsehoods, which among others, may include:

A- Has greatly influenced the socio-economic backwardness, the paths and the wickedness of the same.

B- It is also true that in essence the human socio-economic operation is based on class struggle, for in reality, this operation is part of a graduated scale where the vectors of separation and conflict as sectarian factors are placed both right and left.

C- It is totally false that anyone who enjoys economic prosperity, is a ruthless capitalist, or complicit in this, because in reality on the wealthy to operate within regenerative margins of capitalism, and also practice charity and philanthropy.

D- Is not true that all individuals are behind socially and economically incapable of "breaking a plate and kill a fly", since on the evidence which fully demonstrated that not only can break a set of dishes, but can also kill millions Humans, themselves, accept and celebrate complicity or is made in terms of them.

E- On what elements of proof by which it is shown that the real motivation of the ideologues of the dialectic, is the envy they felt for luxury, comfort and power of the cruel capitalist right, and that the course laggards love was nothing more than an excuse to achieve their goals, and which were still subject to the same to all sorts of hardships.

The dialectical leftists believe that nobody should make more than poverty level, because any excess above that level would make him a cruel capitalist will be stealing the surplus to the poor, and thus: no one, no one should produced in excess, but that still, no one should produce their own, proposing or rather, emerging as one solution: that production must be fully in state hands, which would make "the people" would be the owner, which is nothing else but to say, that production can only be handled in the form of state monopoly by the cruel capitalist of leftism.

In this respect we can say that in appearance, for the capitalists of leftism cruel, truly cruel is the ownership of the means of production, but not the ego, lust and power generating handle such media, and especially morbid generated when operating as their own something that is not forged, which makes it sometimes appear to be free care for the private possession of some means of production and some properties of great value, when in reality on the evidence which shows that if property owners to build their behalf, or through the figure of the figureheads, including this, wealth in secret accounts.

One of the factors that motivates the cruel capitalist of leftism, it stands for, what is striking that seize power and the means of production of others, using simple ideological ruses, which also makes it very ironic how they have been misled so far the ideal factors of center and right, then there is every reason contextual and echo, to give absolute discretion to freedom and the private management of the capital, there are still gaps sovereign knowledge of such reasons and facts, it also Ironically, being readily available the necessary corrections, they find it unrealistic to access them, but not impossible but irony.

In fact the whole ideological factor is extremely ironic, because of the extremely simple solutions are the contextual entanglements, and how extremely difficult it has so far achieved results, and the height of human misery would be a see available solutions, to renege on them, and indeed most of the human operation is so full of clutter and confusion of all kinds, where to get any solutions to sometimes look very difficult, sometimes impossible utopian other, but once collected these solutions , as it is very easy to accept, it is sometimes impossible utopian other, but what if it is very widespread, is that once established the solutions, there are plenty who say that they had achieved the same, how did he not have discovered it?, to discover that it is not science, etc.

You can say that anyone who has planned to build a cultural heritage, moral and economic among others, and do not take into consideration all preventive and corrective parameters with respect to the threats of the cruel capitalist practically be forged that heritage to them, but not for themselves, or their legitimate heirs, relatives, especially if the builder was not willing to risk everything on, in case of imminent danger, in this case this individual would be forging their assets to go to give the hands of neo bastards cruel, that is, of individuals having no relationship of consanguinity or affinity with the owner, seeking to take advantage of loopholes shysters to seize foreign assets or inheritance, and this includes the so-called gold diggers that make life wherever there is money these factors as they could be neutralized by a rigid policy of equity-oriented login or succession only to blood factors, both in life and after their death.

Both neo cruel bastards, as its variant of fortune seekers, cruel capitalists, and common criminals, and all sorts of opportunistic act like rats, that is: as these small rodents that swarm in some homes and that we care about stealing food for the families of those homes, including newborns, as long as they seek to bring food to their young and themselves, and in these cases, both the mother rat to mice children, overflowing in joy for having completed the belly, regardless of the trauma in homes wrecked by the theft, these rodents act without awareness of the harm caused, but not the opportunist, and instead, sometimes acting with great knowledge of the damage caused and that fills them of curiosity and complacency.

Still, the extremist leaders, both left and right, try to train their peers leading them toward higher ruthlessness parameters, so they are very difficult to feel any remorse for the evil they cause, and at the same time feel penchant for evil, being the most common, a taste pathological lying, and once involved or believe to be evil, then begins to operate the law of the underworld, making them slaves of the leaders of the underworld. Both factors also use traditional military training techniques that teach you lose the fear of dying and killing.

In the right-wing extremism, cruelty is training, I was to make them feel that the high socioeconomic status have the "privileged" race to which they belong, and some other factors of distinction and prestige, they find grounds for crush the weak factors counted according to the established order, and we recommend you try hard at those weak and lagging, otherwise it would become the talk back, is more: they see that people like is that try so hard, if not: do not recognize any authority. Among the factors of distinction and prestige, come to light: apart from the social and economic power, the racial, political also on their side, strong ties to the religious than academic and titled nobility, almost all of these factors of power inherently act: and in the socio-economic environment made up the so-called bourgeoisie, and political and religious: the oligarchy, or rule by the few.

In the left-wing extremism, cruelty training practically is to promote some parameters of the antithesis of the ideal of right, but care must be equal or worse than cruel, but almost always framed in two ways: a vengeful marginality and another supreme honor. Marginality by revenge, we seek a claim because of the trauma suffered as a result of attacks from the cruelty of hegemonic right, so use the term inclusion, participation, equality, freedom, etc. To penetrate or eradicate all sectors where there was real or perceived exclusion, unable to participate, inequality, slavery, oppression, tyranny, etc. But the most notable of all this, is the cruelty with which they act, where the principles of forgiveness, compassion, humanity and consideration, seem not to exist.

Through the supreme honor, seeks training in cruelty, trying to monopolize for themselves all that is synonymous with virtue and honor, especially around the main leader of the reason I revolution, this emphasizes attempts at a kind of halo holy and immaculate of such a leader, supposedly incapable of committing any error, both to do good things, and to avoid making the bad, it also presents him as a liberator of the oppressed people, that it was impossible to escape the oppression of slavery, and as one who knows everything that people should or not, whether this term as a national entity or as a laggard sector, and above all: respect for a leader of such a nature would have to give their lives to defend it if necessary , since there never will be another leader so great and perfect as that, although most of the time is seeking to take his life without any remorse for those who dissent from them.

It is common to both left and right sectors, is worth a factor "supporting" it very emblematic figurehead or flag of war, through which lead the attack: in the case of the right, the supporting factor was often represented by the right of conquest, imperial glory, socioeconomic and racial supremacy, the military prestige, etc., while the left supporting factor was often represented by or will, freedom, liberation, revolution, equality, inclusion, nationalism, etc..Also echo some figures of honor and dignity, as in cases where much of the fight, would focus on expelling foreign factors that have turned the nation into a brothel, etc.

After all this tricky spell, hides what they really seek to both leaders cast as the neo capitalist bastards followers and is not nothing but excuses for outright ownership of the entire nation at the cost of any price in lost lives human and material goods, and at least on the evidence that can say without doubt that much of the legacy left and still intends to leave the leftist ideal is a legacy of death, hatred, theft and pain.

Another of the mistakes made by left-dialectical, it represents the fact that the wonders imagine creative and productive capitalists observed in right-center and could continue succeeding with state capitalism, and this is a terrible lack of perspective and knowledge of the natural conditions of the individual and human developed behavior because the individual with his rare exceptions, is by nature seek to get the most out of what is proper, and once the capitalist factor reached own life, the natural conditions of the individual began to reassert itself, towards the possibility of achieving greater economic benefits for themselves through the exploitation of any factor that can capitalize on being among the most successful, those that represent a new mass use and outstanding physical attributes.

The novel factors have much inherent, because apart from the novelty of this or that if compounded factor, almost always generate parameters which need a license or permit use by third factors, and these: those who get the scoop on such concessions, combined with the innovative represent initial, another factor that is typically achieved great social and economic leadership, and can say without falling into any cost, the vast majority of dealers have the gift of making money so I start to do so pay , while the innovative capitalized factor generally has the gift of intelligence and strong hegemonic factor, and the gift of money as an inherent factor.

If there were a large horizon of economic opportunities, innovative intelligence, it would not appeal to innovate, if the fruit of their work did not generate the economic wealth by capitalizing get free, makes innovative intelligence environments capitalism free market is extremely rich in quality and quantity, which has enabled major developmental parameters were observed in countries where both factors coexist, and even better if there is also a central government scheme, except when China, which has begun to have problems because they have a leftist government scheme.

Capitalist supply only encourages innovative minds, but also to almost every type of guy, so much so, that the dream of almost every poor person, is to become rich some day, or at less economically secure a keep it away from the calamities that usually surround poverty, so the cruel capitalist leftists: do nothing but dream truncated welfare of the poor, the limits on the possibilities of living in an environment of free market capitalism In contrast, the leaders of the leftist, if incurred to them, the exclusivity of a life full of power, comfort, wealth, security, cajoling, etc.

Factors innovative intelligence reproached leftist calling it inhumane and only seek what they call the dirty money, but the innovative intelligence ignored them by both the solvency which represents free market capitalism, and to know that leftists reproached only what actually prefer just for them, which was none other things than the dirty money in exchange for crumbs for innovators. Factors right, if you will: they were lovers of innovative intelligence, and were generally willing to pay almost any price to gain access to innovations in science and in art, but eventually chose to deny these innovative, the cruelty to the factors behind, and because they felt that the most logical thing that they take control of your news.

Once the innovative smart assumed to be masters of almost the entire process of capitalizing on their innovations: they did, this has allowed for example: the vast majority of corporate private equity in the hands of innovators I title capitalized factor to which they belong or exploit, this allows a high level and quality of life of people, unfortunately: the leaders of innovative intelligence lapses committed an oversight or strategic, to overturn almost all of its operational capability, encourage the development economic and technological, severely neglecting the ideological factor, while simultaneously lay siege left factors, this has resulted in the present, many corporate groups and indistinct importance capitalists, have been stripped of their heritage by the cruel capitalist left with his followers, the rats of neo bastardism cruel.

The cruel capitalist leftism, with cruel neobastardas rats are almost equal numbers that citizens of order, but because of violent attacks and hoaxes, in some cases the leftists get majority in a democratic election and almost always type in correlated 60% to 40%, it has allowed the proliferation of a major leftist presence of factors in several places in the world, mainly in Latin America, where we have been severely affected only those directly but also indirectly countries with governments center and free-market capitalism, and both nations large and powerful as small nations in these cases, the traumas are generated through economic attacks, mainly from expropriation, nationalization and extortion energy, together with fits of shame, etc. . And let's say this happens: the aberration of longer accept the mere quantitative factor discriminated against qualitative factor to decide the destiny of every nation.

In summary we can say that much of the human operation is based on a correlation of attacks and counterattacks, generated all of them, from different levels of perfections and imperfections, and different motivations, being the most common, desires, needs and circumstances where, if solutions or definitions favorable effects to a harmonic correlation, then the tendency of such operators is to perfection and to the extent of the power of the operators and the different parameters of deliberation that come into play In contrast, if results go against harmonic correlation, then the tendency of these operators is to imperfection.

Regardless of attack and counterattack factors, there are only two factors or poles that surround the others, which are the good and evil, where the regency is good, and acting in its very essence, and the opposite pole or enemy, represents evil, usually acting furtively as if the well, using what we call intellectual defeat, and except for some occasions like common criminals and others, the evil is presented as such and in its own essence, that is, those evil attempt to establish that they are acting as evil, and based on such parameters of perversity present their demands. Sometimes the good acts as if it were evil, but in relative terms, this is the case quiet intelligence, in this perhaps the intelligence agent infiltrated evil factors enter as if part of them, but in reality, this operation it is intended to fight on the basis of the property.

Another factor that usually do good or have the desire to do so, are involved in incidental carelessness, accident or wrongly handled the context of the good, and somehow or other parameters makes them play bad, and almost all of these cases apply parameters of indulgence, according to the absolute right context, but not always in the order established or simple eyes of some, let alone for legal rigorous system, which includes even the death penalty for some types of carelessness or omissions and all these, the most significant is incomplete or incorrect handling of the context good, because usually handle any of its three parameters, but separately and without the proper hierarchy of them, the first and highest ranking:

1 - Practicing exclusively either no decisive impact, directly or evil.

2 - Do not do evil. This is also a way to do good, but are taken into account in a direct and decisive parameters of evil to be avoided on the basis of good, and in this case parameters are not necessarily good or counter-attack of evil, only parameters that could induce temptation to generate a deviation from what is good and fall into what is bad, so this parameter can be defined as equal to not fall into temptation.

3 - Fighting evil. In this case, do good, contract even preemptively if necessary, to the attacks of evil. The well is not a factor attacker, and when it appears to attack, is imperfect, but essentially the context of the good, which happens about the same with evil, for when he apparently does something good, is for involuntary or seeking a deception. In any case, the contexts are absolute as such, but not necessarily the individuals who practice one or another factor, and that human motives, it is virtually impossible to have the complete compendium of the myriad of parameters that apply in each case, which makes the status of each individual, apply by counting between good and evil that will eventually practice and the extent of right or wrong that it would.

All three parameters form a single context, but commonly, through ignorance, it handles only one of them as the context of the good, and also handled the most dissimilar concepts as the definition of good, but such definitions are in fact inherent in the well and Therefore, for the three parameters that make absolute the unique context of the goods, is also good to keep in mind that the context of the property does not apply only in the three parameters as such, but also in the hierarchy of each, which apply in the order given, bearing in mind that ultimately would only fully operational in the first, or exclusively to the well, while the other two, will maintain its absolute quality, but at very low operational profile for reason for the eradication of evil to a minimum, at least in the present system of things.

Motivated to very large and often diffuse bibliography is almost impossible to name them all, in any case: could be included in future editions of these references that in common agreement apply as feasible and needed. Still, it deserves special mention the book by the same author: The Ultimate Logic, copyright 2007